© HAPPINESS SWINGS
BY SANDEEP RAVIDUTT SHARMA

Table of Contents

Introduction IV

Happiness Swings...1

© HAPPINESS SWINGS
BY SANDEEP RAVIDUTT SHARMA

Introduction

This book provides you with a list of **100 motivational quotes and thoughts** focussing mainly on improving your wellness quotient. The positive thoughts bring inner peace and calm. Amazing thoughts are vital to achieving success and happiness in your life. **Happiness swings up and down with you.** All you have to do is hold the chain of positivity with excitement in your heart and smile on your face. This book is just a small attempt to swing happiness in your favour through positive and motivational quotes written with the grace and blessings of **Maa Bhairavi**.

I'm sure if you keep reading, referring, sharing these thoughts and quotes, you may derive inspiration and develop a good understanding of various perspectives and facts about life. I sincerely hope, you will find this book amazing, interesting, rejuvenating, unique and constant source of inspiration.

Thank You and Happy Reading.

© HAPPINESS SWINGS
BY SANDEEP RAVIDUTT SHARMA

© Copyright 2018 Sandeep Ravidutt Sharma - All rights reserved.

In no way is it legal to reproduce, duplicate, or transmit any part of this document in either electronic means or in printed format. Recording of this publication is strictly prohibited and any storage of this document is not allowed unless with written permission from the publisher. All rights reserved. The information provided herein is stated to be truthful and consistent, in that any liability, in terms of inattention or otherwise, by any usage or abuse of any policies, processes, or directions contained within is the solitary and utter responsibility of the recipient reader. Under no circumstances will any legal responsibility or blame be held against the author / publisher for any reparation, damages, or monetary loss due to the information herein, either directly or indirectly. The author own all copyrights.

Legal Notice:
This book is copyright protected. This is only for personal use. You cannot amend, distribute, sell, use, quote or paraphrase any part or the content within this book without the consent of the author or copyright owner. Legal action will be pursued if this is breached.

Disclaimer Notice:
Please note the information contained within this book is for motivational, educational and knowledge sharing purpose only. Every attempt has been made to provide the reader accurate, up to date and reliable complete information. No warranties of any kind are expressed or implied. Readers acknowledge that the author is not engaging in the rendering of legal, financial, medical or professional advice. By reading this document, the reader agrees that under no circumstances the author / publisher is responsible for any losses, direct or indirect, which are incurred as a result of the use of information contained within this document, including, but not limited to, —errors, omissions, or inaccuracies.

If you have further questions, contact on
Tel: +919969256731
Email: sandeepraviduttsharma@gmail.com

© HAPPINESS SWINGS
BY SANDEEP RAVIDUTT SHARMA

Dedication

This book is dedicated to **Goddess Bhairavi**. In the Hindu religion, the Goddess Bhairavi represents divine anger and wrath which is directed towards impurities within us as well as to the negative forces that obstructs our spiritual growth. Bhairavi Mata is also called as **Shubhamkari** and does good things. She is often depicted in images as holding a book, rosary and making abhaya and varada mudra with her hands. She is fiercely protective, lending us wisdom and power, steadiness and clarity. She personifies light and fire, supporting us to reveal what we keep hidden and inviting us to explore our hidden mind and any secret darkness.

I hereby recite the following Bhairavi mool mantra...
"Om Hreem Bhairavi Kalaum Hreem Svaha"
And pray to **Goddess Bhairavi** for lending wisdom and power, steadiness and clarity in the life of my readers and the world. May Goddess Bhairavi protect us from negative forces along with removing impurities of our mind.

HAPPINESS SWINGS

© HAPPINESS SWINGS
BY SANDEEP RAVIDUTT SHARMA

Don't shy away when it's your turn, to tell the truth.

© **HAPPINESS SWINGS**
BY SANDEEP RAVIDUTT SHARMA

At times you need someone to remind that you have reached your destination.

HAPPINESS SWINGS
BY SANDEEP RAVIDUTT SHARMA

Heaven descends on earth when you smile and feel happy. Keep smiling and be happy.

Before you make attempt to know someone, don't begin your probe with a doubt.

If you are not in love with your own self, how can you justify your love for others?

© **HAPPINESS SWINGS**
BY SANDEEP RAVIDUTT SHARMA

The direction and time you choose in your life to go ahead decides about your future.

© HAPPINESS SWINGS
BY SANDEEP RAVIDUTT SHARMA

A straight road may not always lead you to your destination. Be ready to face the twist and turns in your life.

© **HAPPINESS SWINGS**
BY SANDEEP RAVIDUTT SHARMA

Be thankful to the Lord that your dreams have become reality. There are many others who don't even get enough sleep to dream.

© HAPPINESS SWINGS
BY SANDEEP RAVIDUTT SHARMA

To blame it on others is not what winners do.

© **HAPPINESS SWINGS**
BY SANDEEP RAVIDUTT SHARMA

Do what you love and just love what you do. But remember the key is, 'Do'...

© HAPPINESS SWINGS
BY SANDEEP RAVIDUTT SHARMA

Are you waiting for someone to tell you that the celebration is on? The celebration of life has started already on the day you were born.

Drive your good desires towards fulfilment by practicing Karma.

© HAPPINESS SWINGS
BY SANDEEP RAVIDUTT SHARMA

Even thought of thoughtlessness is a thought. Doing nothing is still doing something. What you see is the truth, and what is invisible to you is also true.

Be in the spotlight but for good reasons.

© HAPPINESS SWINGS
BY SANDEEP RAVIDUTT SHARMA

Your attitude influences the circumstances. Be positive and you will find circumstances favouring you.

Take pride in forging the bond of friendship and eliminating enmity between people with your kind and positive words.

© HAPPINESS SWINGS
BY SANDEEP RAVIDUTT SHARMA

You are the richest person on earth if your self-esteem is high enough or equivalent to a billionaire.

You're welcome only if you want to try and not when you want to present excuses for your failure.

© HAPPINESS SWINGS
BY SANDEEP RAVIDUTT SHARMA

Be happy with whatever you have decided.

You cannot experience joy and happiness unless you already have experienced the pain and sufferings in life.

© HAPPINESS SWINGS
BY SANDEEP RAVIDUTT SHARMA

Old habits would die down fast if with your strong willpower you can replace them with positive ones.

Don't let anyone or anything change your mind after you have packed your bags to go.

Work and enjoy during the day as if it was your last day.

© **HAPPINESS SWINGS**
BY SANDEEP RAVIDUTT SHARMA

Don't magnify the problem instead focus and burn it with a quick solution.

Those who lose hope look for excuses and think about how to express regrets. Be ready to embrace positivity which makes you work with no regrets.

Time only freezes for the one who departs from this world and not the ones who are living now.

© HAPPINESS SWINGS
BY SANDEEP RAVIDUTT SHARMA

Freedom of expression makes you sing the song of happiness with life playing soothing music in the background.

Fate never waits. With self-belief and positive traits you can influence your fate.

© HAPPINESS SWINGS
BY SANDEEP RAVIDUTT SHARMA

Build bridges and not bullets. Life is beautiful so are you and me.

You can't curtail the freedom of expression in any society. When such an attempt is made by those in power, revolution is born.

© HAPPINESS SWINGS
BY SANDEEP RAVIDUTT SHARMA

Those who shy away at the time of performing are sure to lose. Give your best to win and reserve your shyness when someone asks you for the secret of your success.

© **HAPPINESS SWINGS**
BY SANDEEP RAVIDUTT SHARMA

Every start craves to meet the end but with a smile.

© HAPPINESS SWINGS
BY SANDEEP RAVIDUTT SHARMA

Opportunities are often hidden in difficulties. It's your choice whether to face or run away from these difficulties and reach out to these opportunities.

Time drives you up and the next moment drops you down. Accept your position with a vow to sync with the time.

© HAPPINESS SWINGS
BY SANDEEP RAVIDUTT SHARMA

You can swim to your destination provided thoughts of drowning don't reside in your mind.

© **HAPPINESS SWINGS**
BY SANDEEP RAVIDUTT SHARMA

Going forward refreshes your mind with just the thought of surprises and novelty.

© HAPPINESS SWINGS
BY SANDEEP RAVIDUTT SHARMA

Always be grateful to those who have time for you. Give your time to those who like your company.

© HAPPINESS SWINGS
BY SANDEEP RAVIDUTT SHARMA

Get ready for tomorrow without losing focus on today.

© HAPPINESS SWINGS
BY SANDEEP RAVIDUTT SHARMA

As the Sun rises in the Sky it's time for you to begin your day's journey without carrying any baggage from yesterday. It's a new day filled with hope to achieve the unachievable. You are here to win...Get Set... Go...

© **HAPPINESS SWINGS**
BY SANDEEP RAVIDUTT SHARMA

The freshness in a relationship is lost with the passage of time as you start focussing on the weaker side of your partner and don't remember positive traits which in the first place attracted you. Treat your relationship with the same freshness as you experienced when you were strangers.

Strange things happens when our focus on the present is lost.

Each of us is a unique creation of the Lord. Some of us are not content and happy even after landing on the Moon while there are others who are thrilled and excited to see the Full Moon through their window.

Do not attempt to write your pain with the ink of tears; it will wash away your words but not the pain.

© HAPPINESS SWINGS
BY SANDEEP RAVIDUTT SHARMA

As one enters the phase of prime youth, the first thing most of us does and believes that our parents hardly know much and are outdated. But the fact is the other way round. Respect the experience of your parents and elders before you decide to know all.

You may like others but can't force others to like you in return.

History records those who win or attempted to win but not the ones who remained passive throughout.

Sincere and consistent efforts explain a winner.

Have you reached where you wanted to be in life? If yes! Help others to realise their dreams.

© HAPPINESS SWINGS
BY SANDEEP RAVIDUTT SHARMA

You can find peace even in a crowd. All you have to do is focus on your inner self and forget the world.

The journey of an epic starts from the first word.

Without imagination, there is no innovation.

Others take control of your life when most of the time you are passive.

God makes the way for you. All you need to have is complete faith and trust in the Lord.

Be obsessed with your goals rather than depressed with your life.

© HAPPINESS SWINGS
BY SANDEEP RAVIDUTT SHARMA

Testing time for you can come at the most inopportune moment. Have faith in God, believe in your self and stay strong throughout. The bad times will pass, just look into the window of hope, and you can see a ray of happiness about to enter.

Life goes on even when everyone seems to be ignorant.

© HAPPINESS SWINGS
BY SANDEEP RAVIDUTT SHARMA

Sometimes life puts you in a situation where both the choices are not what you must have desired. Leave it to time and choose any.

© HAPPINESS SWINGS
BY SANDEEP RAVIDUTT SHARMA

Are you happy today than a few years back? If not. Then do some introspection about what went wrong once for all. Remember all those faults you committed and take a vow not to repeat them again. Get ready with a brand-new action plan, consult your gurus, pray and take blessings from the Lord...Keep Going... Success and Happiness awaits you...

© HAPPINESS SWINGS
BY SANDEEP RAVIDUTT SHARMA

You can't do much when someone loves to hate. You still have a chance if someone hates to love as atleast love dominates his/her mind.

© HAPPINESS SWINGS
BY SANDEEP RAVIDUTT SHARMA

You cannot create a mirror image of someone's happiness and use it. You need to work hard and find the image of joy and happiness within yourself.

© **HAPPINESS SWINGS**
BY SANDEEP RAVIDUTT SHARMA

Invest your time in the right people, if you want to lead a winning team.

© **HAPPINESS SWINGS**
BY SANDEEP RAVIDUTT SHARMA

Do you dream to be rich someday? Let's wish and pray to God that your dreams come true. May God bless you with the richness of thoughts, ideas, knowledge, wealth, heart, pure love and sound health.

© HAPPINESS SWINGS
BY SANDEEP RAVIDUTT SHARMA

Don't accumulate your sins to say, 'Sorry', one day and plead for forgiveness. Intentional apologies are no apology at all. Apologize from your heart and you can start your life afresh.

© HAPPINESS SWINGS
BY SANDEEP RAVIDUTT SHARMA

You earn with your breath in and spend the same with breath out. There is no balance in your life's account when you leave. Stay positive. Take a deep breath in, pause or hold the breath for a while then release your breath. Life never stops... keep going is the mantra...

© HAPPINESS SWINGS
BY SANDEEP RAVIDUTT SHARMA

Start with a tiny step now. With consistency and hard work, giant leaps won't be far off.

© HAPPINESS SWINGS
BY SANDEEP RAVIDUTT SHARMA

At first, all destinations seem reachable. Once you start treading and face challenges, the destination seems to be too far and not reachable. During this period, those who still believe in them self and exhibit patience with concerted efforts are the ones who are sure to succeed at the end.

© HAPPINESS SWINGS
BY SANDEEP RAVIDUTT SHARMA

The dazzling world awaits to cheer your brilliance.

You can't be awake and sleep at the same time.

© HAPPINESS SWINGS
BY SANDEEP RAVIDUTT SHARMA

Fortunate are the ones whose parents are there to guide or scold. Respect your parents and take good care of them when they grow old. Age doesn't matter when old is cared by the young.

Noone plays to fail but not everyone understands what it takes to succeed.

Trust works everytime.

Don't spend time finding out what went wrong, rather find out and implement what works for you.

© **HAPPINESS SWINGS**
BY SANDEEP RAVIDUTT SHARMA

Reaching your destination many a time requires active support from many quarters.

Restart in life with enthusiasm if you have got another chance.

© HAPPINESS SWINGS
BY SANDEEP RAVIDUTT SHARMA

Be the change and the Challenger.

When you fail, accept it gracefully and commit to doing better next time.

© HAPPINESS SWINGS
BY SANDEEP RAVIDUTT SHARMA

Make attempt to rise above the things that hardly matters and look for the bigger picture.

© HAPPINESS SWINGS
BY SANDEEP RAVIDUTT SHARMA

At times the goal post seems to be shifting farther no matter what kind of efforts you are putting in. Focus on your journey in the direction of your destination, life would be easy.

Before you decide to face your enemies at least try making friends.

© HAPPINESS SWINGS
BY SANDEEP RAVIDUTT SHARMA

The world is waiting to cheer for you. Blessings of Sky and Sun are already received. It's time to focus and give your best. It's your day today.

Good deeds never go unnoticed.

© **HAPPINESS SWINGS**
BY SANDEEP RAVIDUTT SHARMA

Doing newer things brings both opportunities and threats. Be ready to face whatever comes your way.

Real leaders appreciate criticism because that's the only way such leaders know their shortcomings and are glad to do a course correction.

Pleading ignorance cannot help, only learning can make you successful.

HAPPINESS SWINGS
BY SANDEEP RAVIDUTT SHARMA

When you depend on others to decide for you. You lose your freedom of expression. Sometimes you may like it when your near and dear ones do it for you and feel the decision as one of your own. Don't make it a habit to let others decide for you.

© HAPPINESS SWINGS
BY SANDEEP RAVIDUTT SHARMA

At times being labelled as a stranger are more desirable than becoming a known acquaintance. Most of the time when you talk to a stranger, your thoughts and actions are not influenced, you have respect and curiosity for the other person. It helps to create bonding. The more you start knowing each other, the grading in your mind starts and the freshness of the meeting is replaced by ignoring attitude.

© HAPPINESS SWINGS
BY SANDEEP RAVIDUTT SHARMA

If you are good enough to maintain your lifestyle but don't have anything to donate. Then assume that you are the poorest among your contacts. You can donate time for some cause if not money. If nothing, at least donate words good enough to motivate or boost the morale of others.

© **HAPPINESS SWINGS**
BY SANDEEP RAVIDUTT SHARMA

Visualise your destination and attract growth through dedicated and determined efforts.

© HAPPINESS SWINGS
BY SANDEEP RAVIDUTT SHARMA

Freedom to accept or disregard views of the other is with you. Accept those which your mind and heart agrees.

The world awaits your win. Take rest and get ready to face tomorrow.

© HAPPINESS SWINGS
BY SANDEEP RAVIDUTT SHARMA

Those who follow discipline hardly repent for their karma. Discipline no doubt suppresses your freedom to a great extent but the intention is noble. It helps you to avoid derailment of any kind.

Think about the beauty and not the misery of life.

© HAPPINESS SWINGS
BY SANDEEP RAVIDUTT SHARMA

Skip the values and discipline in life and one falls flat with no helping hand in sight.

© HAPPINESS SWINGS
BY SANDEEP RAVIDUTT SHARMA

Discuss if you have not understood else you may carry the torch during the day.

© HAPPINESS SWINGS
BY SANDEEP RAVIDUTT SHARMA

Being on the right track is not enough, you need to walk or run at the right speed overcoming all kinds of in your pathway to reach your destination in time.

Say it with words or silent expression. The choice is all yours. In case you chose not to express then don't regret later

© HAPPINESS SWINGS
BY SANDEEP RAVIDUTT SHARMA

Golden words even written in black ink remains golden for the mind that understands.

© HAPPINESS SWINGS
BY SANDEEP RAVIDUTT SHARMA

Through humiliation, you can't win a friend. Only mutual respect can ensure a friendly exchange.

HAPPINESS SWINGS
BY SANDEEP RAVIDUTT SHARMA

Think positive with no IFs and BUTs in your thoughts.

© **HAPPINESS SWINGS**
BY SANDEEP RAVIDUTT SHARMA

Your thoughts can make you a King or a Pauper. Live NOW in the real world and accept gracefully who you are.

www.ingramcontent.com/pod-product-compliance
Lightning Source LLC
Chambersburg PA
CBHW070803220526
45466CB00002B/525